The Inventor's Notebook

The Completely Incredible Inspirations & Ideas of a Genius!

Journal Easy

© 2014

www.journaleasy.com – making journal writing effortless

"Life is pretty simple: You do some stuff. Most fails. Some works. You do more of what works. If it works big, others quickly copy it. Then you do something else. The trick is the doing something else."
- Leonardo da Vinci

 Date:

Date:

Date:

Date:

Date:

Date:

Date:

Date:

Date:

Date:

Date:

Date:

Date:

Date:

Date:

"Human subtlety will never devise an invention more beautiful, more simple or more direct than does nature because in her inventions nothing is lacking, and nothing is superfluous."
- Leonardo da Vinci

Date:

Date:

Date:

Date:

Date:

Date:

Date:

Date:

Date:

Date:

Date:

Date:

Date:

Date:

Date:

"Time stays long enough for anyone who will use it."
- Leonardo da Vinci

Date:

Date:

Date:

Date:

Date:

Date:

Date:

Date:

Date:

Date:

Date:

Date:

Date:

Date:

Date:

"Wisdom is the daughter of experience"
- Leonardo da Vinci

Date:

 Date:

Date:

Date:

Date:

Date:

Date:

Date:

Date:

Date:

Date:

Date:

Date:

Date:

Date:

"I have been impressed with the urgency of doing. Knowing is not enough; we must apply. Being willing is not enough; we must do."
- Leonardo da Vinci

Date:

Date:

Date:

Date:

Date:

Date:

Date:

Date:

Date:

Date:

Date:

Date:

Date:

Date:

Date:

"Nature is the source of all true knowledge. She has her own logic, her own laws, she has no effect without cause nor invention without necessity."
- Leonardo da Vinci

Date:

Date:

Date:

Date:

Date:

Date:

Date:

Date:

Date:

Date:

Date:

Date:

Date:

Date:

Date:

"All our knowledge has its origins in our perceptions."
- Leonardo da Vinci

Date:

Date:

 Date:

Date:

Date:

Date:

Date:

Date:

Date:

Date:

Date:

Date:

Date:

Date:

Date:

"Blinding ignorance does mislead us. O! Wretched mortals, open your eyes!"
- Leonardo da Vinci

Date:

Date:

Date:

Date:

Date:

Date:

Date:

Date:

Date:

Date:

Date:

Date:

Date:

Date:

Date:

"Learning never exhausts the mind."

- Leonardo da Vinci

Date:

Date:

Date:

Date:

Date:

Date:

Date:

Date:

Date:

Date:

Date:

Date:

Date:

Date:

Date:

"Although nature commences with reason and ends in experience it is necessary for us to do the opposite, that is, to commence with experience and from this to proceed to investigate the reason."
- Leonardo da Vinci

Date:

Date:

Date:

Date:

 Date:

Date:

Date:

Date:

Date:

Date:

Date:

Date:

Date:

Date:

Date:

"The noblest pleasure is the joy of understanding."
- Leonardo da Vinci

Date:

www.ingramcontent.com/pod-product-compliance
Ingram Content Group UK Ltd.
Pitfield, Milton Keynes, MK11 3LW, UK
UKHW022226230426
12048UKWH00016BA/1092